Celebrate Winter

All About
Winter
Weather

by Kathryn Clay

CAPSTONE PRESS
a capstone imprint

Little Pebble is published by Capstone Press,
1710 Roe Crest Drive, North Mankato, Minnesota 56003
www.capstonepub.com

Library of Congress Cataloging-in-Publication information is
on file with the Library of Congress.
ISBN 978-1-4914-6008-5 (library binding)
ISBN 978-1-4914-6020-7 (paperback)
ISBN 978-1-4914-6032-0 (ebook PDF)

Editorial Credits

Erika L. Shores, editor; Cynthia Della-Rovere, designer;
Tracy Cummins, media researcher; Tori Abraham, production specialist

Photo Credits

Getty Images: LWA/Dann Tardif, 18; iStockphoto: Christopher Futcher,
21, fotostorm, cover; Shutterstock: Dja65, 1, kaczor58, 3, Kletr, 19,
LilKar, 9, Nemar74, 13, Sebastian Knight, 7, sellingpix, Design Element,
V. J. Matthew, 17; Thinkstock: digitalskillet, 5, Fuse, 11, tarczas, 15,
XiXinXing, 20.

Table of Contents

Hello, Winter

Grab a coat.

Put on a hat.

Winter is here!

The air gets colder.

Snowflakes start to fall.

Plants don't grow.

Trees are bare.

Frost covers branches.

Some places stay warm.

Snow doesn't fall.

People wear shorts all year.

Ice and Snow

Brrr! The air is cold.

Rain freezes.

Frozen rain is called sleet.

Streets are icy.

Plows keep streets safe.

They spread salt and sand.

Wind blows snow
all around.
It's a blizzard.

Winter Fun

Lakes can freeze.

Molly goes ice fishing.

Jack plays hockey.

Sophia makes a snowman.

Lily and Layla go sledding.

What will you do in winter?

Glossary

bare—not covered

blizzard—a snowstorm with high winds making it difficult to see

freeze—to turn from liquid (water) to solid (ice)

frost—a layer of ice crystals formed on the ground or other surfaces

plow—a vehicle that clears snow from roads; a plow spreads sand and salt to melt snow and ice; plows are also called snowplows

winter—one of the four seasons of the year; winter is after fall and before spring

Read More

Aloian, Molly. *How Do We Know It Is Winter?* Seasons Close-Up. New York: Crabtree Pub. Co., 2013.

Esbaum, Jill. *Winter Wonderland.* Washington, D.C.: National Geographic Society, 2010.

Ghigna, Charles. *I See Winter.* North Mankato, Minn.: Picture Window Books, 2012.

Internet Sites

FactHound offers a safe, fun way to find Internet sites related to this book. All of the sites on FactHound have been researched by our staff.

Here's all you do:
Visit *www.facthound.com*
Type in this code: 9781491460085

Super-cool stuff! Check out projects, games and lots more at
www.capstonekids.com

Index